WHAT DO YOU KNOW ABOUT

AIDS

PETE SANDERS and STEVE MYERS

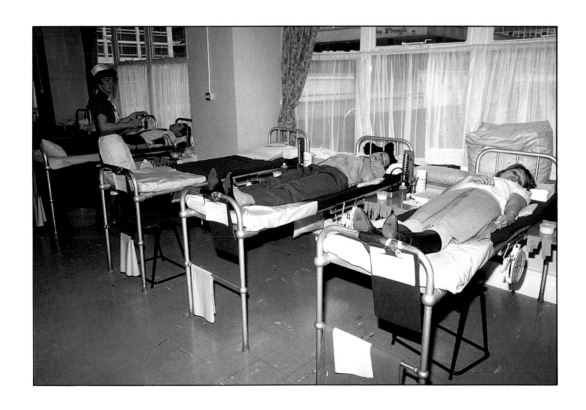

Gloucester Press

LONDON • SYDNEY

An Aladdin Book
© Aladdin Books Ltd 1996

Designed and produced by
Aladdin Books Ltd
28 Percy Street
London W1P 0LD

First published in Great Britain in
1996 by Franklin Watts
96 Leonard Street
London EC2A 4RH

ISBN: 0 7496 2 4795

A catalogue record for this book is
available from the British Library.

Printed in Belgium

Design   David West
                  Children's Book
                  Design
Designer   Ed Simkins
Editor   Alex Edmonds
Picture Research Brooks Krikler
                  Research
Illustrator   Mike Lacey

Pete Sanders is Senior Lecturer in
health education at the University of
North London. He was a head teacher
for ten years and has written many
books on social issues for children.

Steve Myers is a freelance writer. He
has co-written other titles in this series
and has worked on several
educational projects for children.

The consultant, Julie Johnson is a health
education consultant and trainer,
working with children and young
people, parents, teachers, carers and
organisations such as Kidscape.

CONTENTS

HOW TO USE THIS BOOK

The books in this series are intended to help young people to understand more about issues that may affect their lives.

Each book can be read by a child alone, or together with a parent, teacher or helper. Issues raised in the storyline are further discussed in the accompanying text, so that there is an opportunity to talk through ideas as they come up.

At the end of the book there is a section called "What Can We Do?" This gives practical ideas which will be useful for both young people and adults. Organisations and helplines are also listed, to provide the reader with additional sources of information and support.

INTRODUCTION

TODAY, THANKS TO RESEARCH AND EDUCATION, WE KNOW MUCH MORE ABOUT AIDS THAN WE DID JUST A FEW YEARS AGO.

It is an issue which concerns everyone. AIDS is still a very serious health problem, affecting millions of people, and is likely to remain so for some time yet.

This book will explain what AIDS is, how it is transmitted, and the effects the disease can have on people's lives. Each chapter introduces a different aspect of the subject, illustrated by a continuing storyline. The characters in the story have to deal with situations which many people may experience. After each episode, we stop and look at the issues raised, widening out the discussion. By the end you will know the facts about AIDS, have considered attitudes towards the disease and towards the people who have it. You will see how you can protect yourself from the virus.

AIDS TODAY

SINCE THE FIRST CASE WAS IDENTIFIED IN 1979, AIDS HAS BECOME A WORLDWIDE HEALTH PROBLEM, WITH CASES REPORTED ON EVERY CONTINENT, IN MORE THAN 100 COUNTRIES.

However, a great deal of progress has been made in understanding the nature of the disease, and how we can reduce the risk of exposure to the virus which causes it.
Initial reports about AIDS in the media were often misleading or false, causing panic and prejudice. Education measures have helped to counteract this, and make sure people are correctly informed. Many governments are funding research into trying to find a cure for AIDS and a vaccine to prevent the spread of the virus. It could still be many years before a cure is available. As you grow up, you will be making decisions about your life and health. The vast majority of us are likely to be unaffected directly by AIDS, but it is vital to see the need to protect yourself from the virus, and be sensitive to the issues.

AIDS has the potential to be a problem for many different people.

▽The Woodhouse family were having a small party to celebrate the new arrival.

▽The same evening, Lewis Turner and his brother, Waylan, were going out.

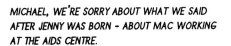

MICHAEL, WE'RE SORRY ABOUT WHAT WE SAID AFTER JENNY WAS BORN - ABOUT MAC WORKING AT THE AIDS CENTRE.

IT DID UPSET US, LIZZIE. WHAT YOU SAID WAS VERY HURTFUL.

I NEED TO BORROW SOME MONEY... HEY, A CONDOM!

LEWIS, GET OUT OF THERE! YOU SHOULDN'T GO INTO OTHER PEOPLE'S PROPERTY.

WE KNOW THAT NOW. ANNA, LET UNCLE MICHAEL HOLD HER.

I DON'T GET IT, WHY ARE YOU CARRYING A CONDOM?

YOU TOLD MUM THAT YOU AND THIS GUY WERE JUST FRIENDS.

WE ARE, NOT THAT IT'S ANY OF YOUR BUSINESS. LOTS OF WOMEN CARRY CONDOMS THESE DAYS.

▽Glen and Anna Woodhouse had arranged to go out with their friends.

WHO SAID JOANNA COULD GO?

SHE'S COMING WITH US.

MAYUMI'S RIGHT. NOBODY ASKED YOU ANYWAY.

WHAT IS YOUR PROBLEM, KIERAN? I DON'T HAVE HIV, I WOULDN'T CATCH IT FROM MY MUM, AND IF I DID, YOU CAN'T GET IT FROM BEING WITH ME.

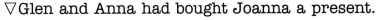

WHETHER YOU COME OR NOT IS UP TO YOU.

▽Glen and Anna had bought Joanna a present.

IT'S AN AIDS AWARENESS RIBBON. IT'S SO THAT PEOPLE DON'T FORGET AIDS.

THANKS. YOU'RE BOTH WEARING ONE TOO. THAT'LL GIVE KIERAN SOMETHING TO THINK ABOUT!

△Kieran went with them. After all that he'd learnt about AIDS from his friends recently, he was starting to feel embarrassed about the things that he'd said.

I HOPE HE REALISES HOW STUPID HE'S BEEN. WE'VE ALL LEARNED A LOT THESE LAST FEW MONTHS.

Some people now feel, wrongly, that AIDS is no longer an important issue.
This is because the number of people affected by AIDS has not reached the level predicted when it was first identified in some countries. Some people wear AIDS awareness ribbons like the one Glen gave Joanna. The ribbons tell people that AIDS is still a very serious problem.

We all have a part to play in informing others, challenging prejudice and working to find a cure.

Many young people wonder what AIDS has to do with them.
As you grow into an adult, the choices you make about your lifestyle and the relationships you enter into can have a direct effect on your health and future. The more you know at an early stage about all the issues involved, the easier it will be for you to protect yourself, and to make informed decisions when the time comes.

One important focus of AIDS education is the issue of 'safer sex'.
This is something which may not concern you right now. But it is a subject you will need to know about when you are older, and sexually active. Whilst sex is not dangerous in itself, sexual activity can carry a risk of passing on the AIDS virus from one partner to the other. Many adults as well as young people recognise the importance of having a responsible attitude towards sexual activities.

WHAT IS AIDS?

AIDS STANDS FOR 'ACQUIRED IMMUNE DEFICIENCY SYNDROME'. IT IS A CONDITION WHICH MAKES THE BODY UNABLE TO FIGHT DISEASE.

When you are ill it is your immune system – your body's defence against disease – which comes into play to make you better again. HIV, the virus that causes AIDS, works by attacking the immune system itself.

Your immune system can recognise thousands of possible disease-causing organisms and will act immediately to fight off any bacteria or virus which does get into the body. This is called the 'immune response', and is controlled by special white cells in your blood. The most important ones are called lymphocytes. There are two kinds: B-cells and T-cells. B-cells produce chemicals which lock on to an invader and prevent it attacking other cells. T-cells attack and kill foreign organisms directly. They also regulate the workings of the whole immune system, and are therefore vital to good health. HIV destroys these cells, usually over many years, leaving the body increasingly vulnerable to infection and illness. It is widely accepted that this immune deficiency will eventually prove fatal, although many people now live with AIDS for many years.

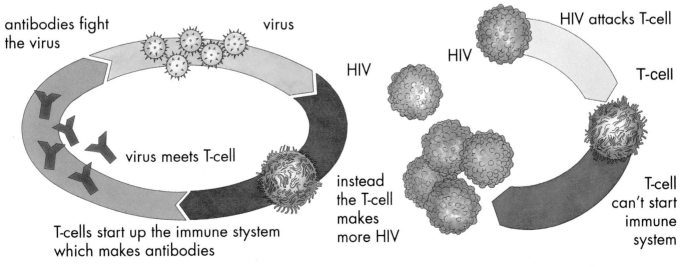

antibodies fight the virus

virus

virus meets T-cell

T-cells start up the immune stystem which makes antibodies

HIV

instead the T-cell makes more HIV

HIV

HIV attacks T-cell

T-cell

T-cell can't start immune system

showing how the immune system works normally

showing how HIV attacks the immune system

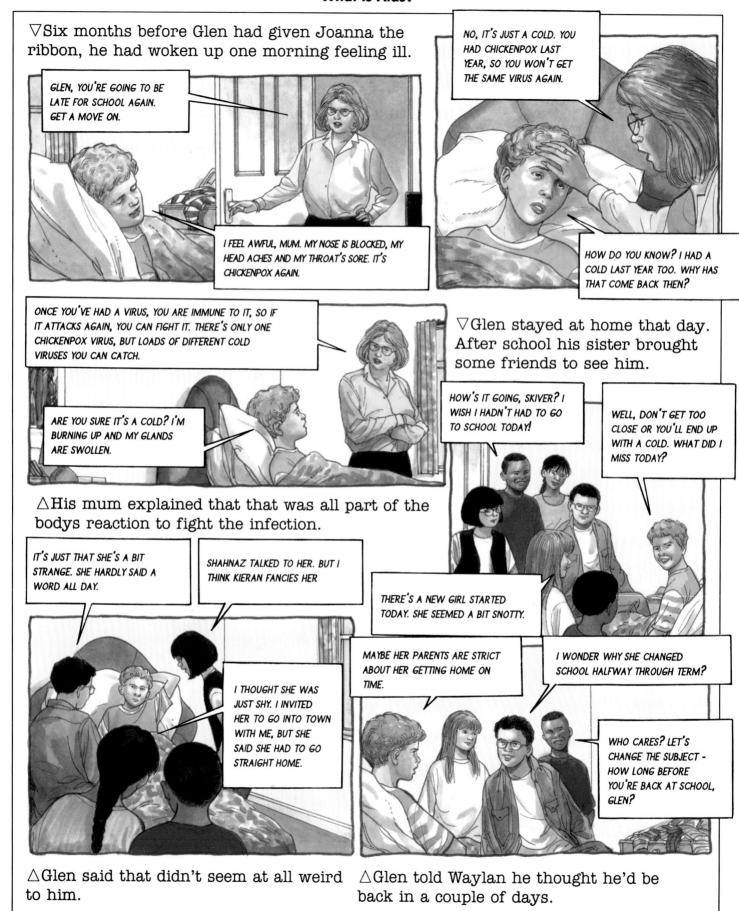

▽Six months before Glen had given Joanna the ribbon, he had woken up one morning feeling ill.

GLEN, YOU'RE GOING TO BE LATE FOR SCHOOL AGAIN. GET A MOVE ON.

I FEEL AWFUL, MUM. MY NOSE IS BLOCKED, MY HEAD ACHES AND MY THROAT'S SORE. IT'S CHICKENPOX AGAIN.

NO, IT'S JUST A COLD. YOU HAD CHICKENPOX LAST YEAR, SO YOU WON'T GET THE SAME VIRUS AGAIN.

HOW DO YOU KNOW? I HAD A COLD LAST YEAR TOO. WHY HAS THAT COME BACK THEN?

ONCE YOU'VE HAD A VIRUS, YOU ARE IMMUNE TO IT, SO IF IT ATTACKS AGAIN, YOU CAN FIGHT IT. THERE'S ONLY ONE CHICKENPOX VIRUS, BUT LOADS OF DIFFERENT COLD VIRUSES YOU CAN CATCH.

ARE YOU SURE IT'S A COLD? I'M BURNING UP AND MY GLANDS ARE SWOLLEN.

△His mum explained that that was all part of the bodys reaction to fight the infection.

▽Glen stayed at home that day. After school his sister brought some friends to see him.

HOW'S IT GOING, SKIVER? I WISH I HADN'T HAD TO GO TO SCHOOL TODAY!

WELL, DON'T GET TOO CLOSE OR YOU'LL END UP WITH A COLD. WHAT DID I MISS TODAY?

IT'S JUST THAT SHE'S A BIT STRANGE. SHE HARDLY SAID A WORD ALL DAY.

SHAHNAZ TALKED TO HER. BUT I THINK KIERAN FANCIES HER

THERE'S A NEW GIRL STARTED TODAY. SHE SEEMED A BIT SNOTTY.

I THOUGHT SHE WAS JUST SHY. I INVITED HER TO GO INTO TOWN WITH ME, BUT SHE SAID SHE HAD TO GO STRAIGHT HOME.

MAYBE HER PARENTS ARE STRICT ABOUT HER GETTING HOME ON TIME.

I WONDER WHY SHE CHANGED SCHOOL HALFWAY THROUGH TERM?

WHO CARES? LET'S CHANGE THE SUBJECT - HOW LONG BEFORE YOU'RE BACK AT SCHOOL, GLEN?

△Glen said that didn't seem at all weird to him.

△Glen told Waylan he thought he'd be back in a couple of days.

Glen feels ill because of a cold virus.

Viruses are tiny organisms, so small they can only be seen using a microscope. When a virus attacks cells in the body, it changes the way the cell works and makes thousands of copies of itself. The new viruses go on to infect surrounding cells. This is where the immune system will usually spring into action. AIDS is caused by a virus called HIV.

The cells in Glen's bloodstream are working to fight the cold virus.

The chemicals produced by the B-cells are called antibodies. They lock on to the virus and stop it destroying other cells. Each antibody works on only one kind of virus, so a healthy body is capable of producing thousands of different antibodies. People who have AIDS can eventually lose the ability to produce the necessary antibodies to fight any other virus or bacteria which invades the body.

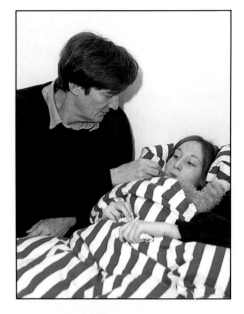

Mrs Woodhouse is not worried about Glen feeling ill. She knows that he can't have caught chickenpox again because his body is already protected against the illness.

Once your body has produced antibodies to fight an infection, it can make them again very quickly if the same infection reoccurs. You then become immune to that particular bacteria or virus. Vaccines – medicines which give immunity to certain diseases – work by introducing a weak strain of a virus into the bloodstream, so that the body begins to produce the necessary antibodies to fight the virus or infection*.

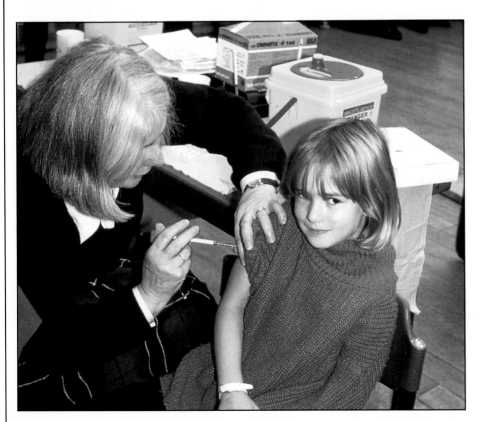

THE HIV VIRUS

THE HUMAN IMMUNODEFICIENCY VIRUS, OR HIV, IS THE ORGANISM WHICH CAUSES AIDS.

However, HIV does not always attack the immune system immediately. It may remain in the bloodstream for many years without a person showing any signs of illness.
When HIV first gets into the blood the body produces antibodies to try to fight the invader. However, HIV constantly changes its composition. This makes the body believe it is no longer there. It can then 'hide' inside cells which the body thinks are still healthy. When it starts attacking the immune system, it can make copies of itself more quickly than any other known virus. It infects the T-cells fooling them into attacking other healthy T-cells. Someone who is infected with the virus, but whose immune system has not yet been attacked would be termed 'HIV positive'. Once the immune system has been destroyed, a person is sometimes referred to as having 'full-blown AIDS'.

A blood test is available to find out if HIV is in the body.

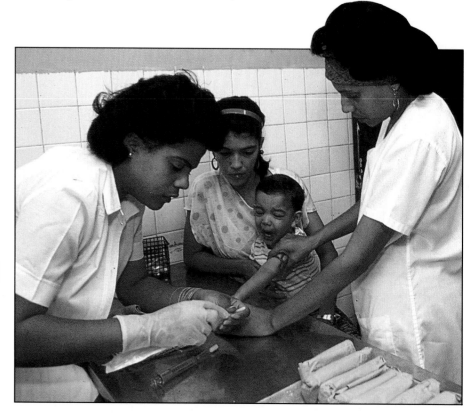

▽The following Sunday, Glen and Anna went round to their Uncle Michael's house.

▽Mac was Michael's friend. They had shared a house for seven years.

PUT SOME MUSIC ON IF YOU LIKE, GLEN. HOW'S YOUR COLD? ARE YOU FEELING BETTER NOW?

MUCH BETTER THANKS. WHERE'S MAC? I THOUGHT HE WAS GOING TO BE HERE.

HE'LL BE HOME SOON. HE'S WORKING AT THE CALLEN CENTRE, AND HE HAS TO WORK SUNDAYS.

THAT'S A PLACE FOR PEOPLE WITH AIDS ISN'T IT? ISN'T HE AFRAID HE'LL CATCH IT?

YOU CAN'T 'CATCH' AIDS LIKE YOU CATCH A COLD. IT DOESN'T TRAVEL THROUGH THE AIR.

▽Michael said he and Mac had been tested for the virus, and were negative.

MAC REALLY FELT THAT HE WANTED TO DO SOMETHING TO HELP. IT'S NOT AS IF IT'S RISKY IF HE AVOIDS CONTACT WITH BLOOD OR BODILY FLUIDS FROM PEOPLE WITH HIV.

SO MAC CAN'T GET IT THEN FROM GOING TO THE CENTRE.

I THINK HE'S REALLY BRAVE DOING THAT, IT MUST BE VERY STRESSFUL.

WHAT EXACTLY DOES THAT MEAN?

IT MEANS THEY DON'T HAVE AIDS!

IT ACTUALLY MEANS THAT THE HIV VIRUS WHICH CAUSES AIDS ISN'T IN OUR BLOODSTREAM.

▽Mac got home later feeling sad. A patient had died that morning.

I'M SORRY MAC, WAS HE YOUR FRIEND?

MICHAEL AND I HAVE KNOWN HIM FOR YEARS. HE WAS DOING OKAY UNTIL HE GOT PNEUMOCYSTIS.

WHAT'S THAT? I THOUGHT HE HAD AIDS?

HE DID. HIV DESTROYS THE IMMUNE SYSTEM, SO OTHER DISEASES ATTACK. PNEUMOCYSTIS IS A SEVERE FORM OF PNEUMONIA.

IT MUST BE AWFUL SEEING THAT HAPPEN TO FRIENDS.

IT IS - BUT I GET A LOT OF SATISFACTION WORKING AT THE CENTRE. IT ISN'T ALL DOOM AND GLOOM.

△Mac said that the people at the centre were just trying to get on with their lives.

Michael and Mac have both tested negative for the HIV virus.
This test detects antibodies to HIV in the blood. This tells the doctor that the virus must be present. Of course, HIV and AIDS do not only affect a person's physical health. Coming to terms with the result of a positive HIV test can be emotionally very difficult, and people should be offered counselling before and after a test.

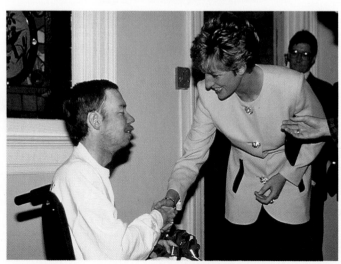

Mac's friend with AIDS has died from an unusual form of pneumonia.
People with full-blown AIDS are vulnerable to many diseases. Many suffer from severe diarrhoea, fever, cancers and extreme weight loss. Some diseases are very rare, and had not been seen in humans before.

HIV can cause other problems as well.
HIV also affects the nervous system, and may cause memory loss and depression. A person can be HIV postive and not show any symptoms of disease for many years.

HOW DO PEOPLE GET AIDS?

PEOPLE DO NOT 'CATCH' AIDS IN THE SAME WAY THEY MIGHT A COLD.

For infection to occur, the virus has to pass directly into the bloodstream. This means HIV can only be passed on in certain special ways.

Very small amounts of HIV are enough to infect someone. Anyone carrying the virus has the potential to pass it on to another person, even if she or he still appears perfectly healthy. HIV is only present in blood and blood products. The most common way for the virus to be transmitted is through the sharing of bodily fluids. This might be during sex, with infected sperm or vaginal fluid being passed from one person to another. Sharing needles for injecting drugs is highly risky, as tiny amounts of blood can be trapped in the end of the needle. Pregnant women who are HIV positive can also pass the virus to their unborn child, and there have been cases reported of HIV being passed on through breastfeeding. It is not carried in waste products such as urine or sweat.

HIV and AIDS cannot be passed on by casual day to day contact with an infected person.

Joanna knows you can only contract the HIV virus from an infected person.
There is no way of telling whether a person has the virus or not. People may not even know themselves. This is why it is important not to expose yourself to any risk.

Shahnaz says people have contracted HIV from blood transfusions.
Before it was understood that AIDS was caused by a virus which was present in blood, the blood used in transfusions was not checked. This led to some people being given HIV infected blood, and developing AIDS. Now all blood donations are checked to make sure they are safe. There is absolutely no risk of contracting the virus by giving blood.

HIV can be passed on in sperm or vaginal fluids.
Many people use condoms as a responsible option if they are going to have a sexual relationship. They prevent sperm from entering the other persons body, and reduce the risk of infection, although they do not take it away completely. Both men and women may chose to carry them.

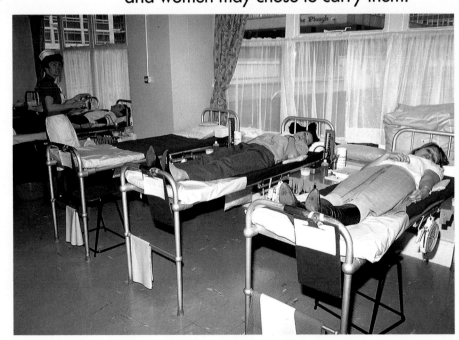

WHO IS AFFECTED BY AIDS?

IT CAN BE TEMPTING TO BELIEVE THAT HIV AND AIDS ARE OTHER PEOPLE'S PROBLEMS. IN FACT THE ISSUES CONCERN EVERYONE.

Millions of people are affected by HIV and AIDS. They come from different backgrounds and cultures, and are people just like you or me.

It is hard to know how many people are carrying the HIV virus, since they can stay healthy for many years. When it was first identified in western society, AIDS seemed to affect mostly homosexual men. It soon became apparent that this disease was not a 'gay plague', as some people were calling it. Worldwide most people with the disease are heterosexual. Current evidence suggests that people with HIV or AIDS are men and women, young and old, black and white, heterosexual and homosexual. HIV and AIDS are not something that any one sector of society can afford to ignore. People who have injected drugs also make up a proportion of those affected.

AIDS does not only harm the thousands of men and women with the disease. Family and friends have to deal with difficult situations and emotions too.

▽Glen and Anna's older brother James and his wife had just had a baby.

SHE'S SO TINY, LOOK AT HER HANDS.

SHE'S LOVELY. MICHAEL'S OUTSIDE WITH MAC. I'LL BRING THEM IN TO SEE HER.

I DON'T THINK WE CAN HAVE TOO MANY VISITORS.

HI MICHAEL, MAC. LOOK I DON'T KNOW HOW TO SAY THIS.

HI JAMES, WHAT'S THE MATTER?

IS THE BABY OK? I CAN'T WAIT TO SEE HER.

△James said the baby was fine, but he and Lizzie would prefer it if they didn't go in to see her right now.

WE KNOW MAC'S BEEN WORKING AT THE AIDS CENTRE. I'M SORRY BUT WE'RE WORRIED ABOUT EXPOSING THE BABY TO ANY POSSIBLE RISK. I HATE TO DO THIS, BUT YOU MUST UNDERSTAND.

OH I THINK WE UNDERSTAND. YOU'RE WRONG YOU KNOW.

HE'S RIGHT, THEY CAN'T HARM THE BABY.

JAMES, IT'S ONLY THE WAY YOU BEHAVE THAT CAN PUT YOU AT RISK YOU KNOW. COME ON MAC, LET'S GO.

△They left James who was feeling embarrassed.

▽Anna came out and asked what had happened.

▽The following week, Glen and Anna went round to see Lewis and Waylan.

JAMES WOULDN'T LET MICHAEL AND MAC SEE THE BABY, 'COS HE'S WORRIED ABOUT AIDS.

I DIDN'T MEAN TO UPSET THEM.

WHAT'S GOING ON?

NICOLA'S GOING OUT WITH HER NEW BOYFRIEND. MUM'S TRYING TO HAVE A TALK TO HER, BUT NICOLA ISN'T INTERESTED.

NEITHER OF THEM HAS THE VIRUS. EVEN IF THEY DID HAVE IT, THEY COULDN'T PASS IT ON JUST BY HOLDING THE BABY.

17

△Up in Lewis's room, Waylan said he thought his mum was overreacting.

▷Lewis was realising the impact HIV and AIDS could have on people's lives.

18

Michael says that it is the way you behave that puts you at risk, not who you are.
Some people think of AIDS as affecting only certain sectors of society. This encourages prejudice. What matters is whether you put yourself at risk, not who you are – the AIDS Quilt (above) is made up of the names of people who have died from AIDS. The variety of names shows that HIV and AIDS are a global problem.

It isn't obvious if someone is HIV positive.
This means that people who are starting a sexual relationship need to be able to trust their partners and talk to them. Health and sex education for young people enables them to understand the risks and how they can protect themselves when they are older.

Lewis isn't worried about AIDS.
Growing up you might be faced with temptations which are hard to resist. You may feel 'it won't happen to me', but it is still important to remember that nobody is indestructible when it comes to AIDS.

RESPONSES TO HIV AND AIDS

PEOPLE HAVE A VARIETY OF ATTITUDES TOWARDS HIV AND AIDS AND THOSE PEOPLE WHO ARE AFFECTED BY THEM.

Many realised the need to educate people quickly, and support those affected. Unfortunately some did not respond as positively to the disease. Initially, nobody understood exactly how the virus was spread. This led to some panic, especially when it became clear that AIDS could affect huge numbers of people. Some people had extreme views, such as those that are diagnosed with HIV or AIDS should be locked away. Many people believe that governments acted slowly in coming forward with funds for research into the disease. The complicated nature of the disease and confusion about the way in which it is passed on led to disagreement about how to tell the public about the risks and precisely what to tell them. Many of the details were unclear at first. This has thankfully changed recently. Money is now being spent and conferences about AIDS and HIV are being staged to raise awareness and to discuss the issues. Education messages are getting through, but young people must realise the risks of contracting HIV are still real.

Sometimes people have been very unkind to those with HIV or AIDS, because they do not understand the nature of the disease, and are afraid, wrongly, of being infected.

▽A few weeks later, Glen, Anna and their mum bumped into Mac in town.

HI, THIS IS A FRIEND- PEDRO. WE'VE JUST BEEN SHOPPING FOR A FEW THINGS FOR THE CENTRE.

HI PEDRO. WE'RE ON OUR WAY HOME. THE CENTRE'S ON OUR WAY. WE CAN GIVE THEM A LIFT CAN'T WE MUM?

OF COURSE WE CAN.

▽On the way to the car, Anna asked Pedro how long he'd worked at the Centre.

I DON'T WORK THERE. I RUN A GROUP FOR PEOPLE LIKE ME WHO ARE HIV POSITIVE. WE CAMPAIGN FOR MORE MONEY FOR RESEARCH INTO THE DISEASE.

YOU SHOULD SEE THE HEADLINES PEDRO AND HIS FRIENDS HAVE COLLECTED. SOME OF THE THINGS THE PAPERS SAY ARE RIDICULOUS.

IT'S HARD TO BELIEVE YOU'RE HIV POSITIVE, PEDRO. YOU LOOK SO HEALTHY.

THANKS! I WATCH MY DIET AND TAKE PLENTY OF EXERCISE TO KEEP AS FIT AS POSSIBLE. IT'S IMPORTANT TO KEEP HEALTHY.

◁As they arrived at the centre, Glen spotted someone he knew.

HEY, ISN'T THAT JOANNA? WHAT'S SHE DOING HERE, AND WHO'S THAT WITH HER?

I DON'T KNOW. JOANNA!

THEY SAW US, GRAN. THEY'RE BOUND TO TELL EVERYONE THAT MUM HAS AIDS.

IT'S SO UNFAIR, GRAN. WHY DOES IT HAVE TO BE MUM? I TRY NOT TO CRY FOR HER SAKE, BUT I FEEL SO SAD SOMETIMES. IT SHOULDN'T HAPPEN TO PEOPLE LIKE MUM.

I KNOW. SHE'S YOUR MUM, BUT SHE'S MY DAUGHTER TOO. ANYWAY, AIDS REALLY SHOULDN'T HAPPEN TO ANYONE.

△Anna called out twice, but Joanna didn't respond.

▷That evening at home Joanna was upset.

YOU DON'T KNOW THAT JOANNA, I KNOW IT'S DIFFICULT, BUT DON'T FEEL ASHAMED ABOUT IT.

△Joanna was worried about what would happen at school.

Joanna's gran knows that nobody deserves to have AIDS.

Some people are not as sensitive as Joanna's gran. These people claim that many of those who have the disease have brought it on themselves. This is a very bad attitude and does not solve anything. Blaming people infected with AIDS does not help to cure them. We should fight the virus, not the people who have it.

Some tabloid newspapers used shock headlines to describe AIDS stories.

As Pedro and Mac know, when HIV and AIDS first became news, many items in the media were grossly exaggerated, or simply untrue. They only served to create panic and cause more prejudice. It is often difficult to make sense of some of the things you read and hear. Remember that reports in the media might not give the whole truth, or may only tell you one side of a particular story.

Pedro's group supports people with HIV.

This is an example of the very positive responses to AIDS. Many groups and charities campaign for more money to be spent on research. Others try to improve the way people who are HIV positive or have AIDS are treated, fighting for equal rights for them. Many offer practical help for people with AIDS and their relatives.

LIVING WITH HIV AND AIDS

BEING HIV POSITIVE OFTEN FORCES PEOPLE TO CONSIDER ISSUES OF LIFE AND DEATH WHICH THEY HAD PREVIOUSLY NOT FACED UP TO.

Finding out can be devastating. However, many people come to terms with the diagnosis and live with HIV or AIDS without letting it get in the way of their lives. Some people become determined to get the best out of life for as long as possible. It might mean adopting a slightly different lifestyle – perhaps cutting out alcohol and tobacco, and changing the diet to help the immune system keep healthy. Not everyone copes well with the news, though. Many people don't tell others they are HIV positive, because they are afraid of the reaction. People with HIV may also worry about falling ill, in case it signals the onset of full-blown AIDS. People with AIDS may need to take a variety of drugs, which may have side effects. They may need to go into hospital from time to time to cope with a particular illness. Signs of disease, such as weight loss and blotches on the skin, mean that AIDS can be a very 'public' condition. People may be stared at, or avoided.

As the illness worsens, people may not be able to care for themselves and may need to rely on friends or family much more. This can be very hard.

▽On Monday morning, Joanna didn't want to go to school.

YOU MUST GO TO SCHOOL, DARLING. I'M SURE IT'LL BE FINE. DO YOU WANT ME TO SPEAK TO THE HEADTEACHER?

THEY SAID SUCH AWFUL THINGS ABOUT YOU. NONE OF IT WAS TRUE, BUT THAT DIDN'T STOP THEM. I LOVE YOU, MUM. WHY IS THIS HAPPENING TO US?

NO, MUM. I'M OKAY. I JUST HATE LISTENING TO THEIR STUPID COMMENTS. IT WAS TERRIBLE AT MY LAST SCHOOL, TOO.

▽On the way home, Glen and Anna caught up with Joanna.

I KNOW DARLING. BUT WE'VE BOTH GOT TO BE STRONG. WE'LL GET THROUGH THIS TOGETHER.

▷Joanna went to school. Nobody mentioned anything about her mum all day.

I KNOW, MUM. BUT IT'S REALLY HARD SOMETIMES.

HEY, JOANNA, SLOW DOWN. WE JUST WANTED TO LET YOU KNOW THAT WE'RE NOT GOING TO SAY ANYTHING.

ABOUT WHAT? I DON'T KNOW WHAT YOU'RE TALKING ABOUT.

PLEASE DON'T TELL ANYONE. YOU'VE GOT TO PROMISE.

DON'T WORRY, WE WON'T. WE DON'T WANT TO CAUSE ANY TROUBLE.

WE SAW YOU ON SATURDAY, JOANNA. WAS THAT YOUR MUM YOU WERE WITH?

THERE'S NOTHING TO BE ASHAMED OF.

A FRIEND OF OURS, MAC, WORKS AT THE CENTRE, THAT'S WHY WE WERE THERE. DO YOU KNOW HIM?

I'VE MET HIM A FEW TIMES, HE'S REALLY NICE, AND FUNNY.

△Joanna said she didn't feel ashamed. She said most people just refused to understand the situation.

▷Glen invited Joanna round for something to drink.

HAS YOUR MUM BEEN ILL LONG?

▽Joanna didn't answer at first. Eventually she decided to trust Glen and Anna.

SHE'S HAD FULL-BLOWN AIDS FOR ABOUT A YEAR. MY PARENTS DIVORCED WHEN I WAS EIGHT. THEN MUM MET SOMEONE ELSE. THAT WAS GREAT, UNTIL HE GOT ILL.

WE HAD TO MOVE TO GRAN'S WHEN SHE GOT THE FULL-BLOWN AIDS. SHE'S DOING OKAY. SHE TAKES LOADS OF TABLETS AND STUFF, THOUGH.

I'D REALLY LIKE TO MEET HER.

△Joanna said she'd talk to her mum about them coming round at the weekend.

HERE SHE COMES. DON'T GET TOO CLOSE. HOW'S YOUR MOTHER THESE DAYS?

KIERAN, WHAT ARE YOU TALKING ABOUT?

HER MOTHER'S GOT AIDS. THAT'S HER BIG SECRET.

△One morning Joanna arrived at school to find Kieran waiting for her.

▷Joanna was furious. She ran to find Glen.

▽Joanna said he died almost two years ago. Then her mum found out she was HIV positive too.

I'M SORRY. I CAN'T IMAGINE HOW YOU MUST FEEL.

WHEN PEOPLE FIRST FOUND OUT, I USED TO TELL THEM SHE'D GOT THE VIRUS FROM A BLOOD TRANSFUSION. I THOUGHT IT SOUNDED BETTER.

HOW'S YOUR MUM NOW?

▽A few weeks later, Shahnaz and Mayumi were talking to Anna.

SO WHAT'S GOING ON WITH YOU AND JOANNA? YOU'VE BEEN SPENDING A LOT OF TIME WITH HER.

HAVE YOU FOUND OUT HER SECRET?

WHAT SECRET? JOANNA'S NICE - SHE'S JUST SHY. COME ON, WE'LL BE LATE.

JOANNA, I DIDN'T SAY A WORD, I SWEAR.

YOU MUST HAVE DONE. HOW ELSE WOULD THEY FIND OUT? I CAN'T BELIEVE I TRUSTED YOU.

Glen had promised not to tell anyone that Joanna's mum has AIDS.
Confidentiality is a major HIV and AIDS issue. The results of tests are private, but the decision to tell people of a positive result can be very difficult. People may be scared of others finding out that they have been for a test, because of the way HIV and AIDS are still viewed by some people. It is very important to respect a person's right to confidentiality.

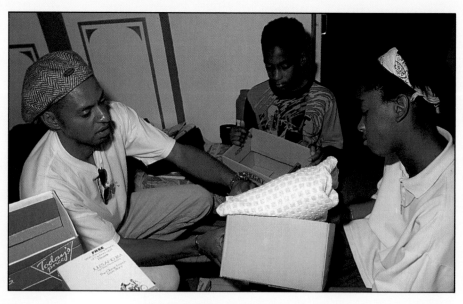

Kieran has been really unkind to Joanna.
Despite all the work which has been done to inform people about AIDS, reactions to the disease itself, as well as to those infected, can still be negative.

Some people have been thrown out of their houses or lost their jobs because they are HIV positive. Instead of receiving the love and support they badly need from their colleagues, friends and family, many have been made to feel ashamed, or have been deserted by their loved ones. Thankfully, this is not always the case, and there have also been good responses.

Joanna's mum has a positive attitude towards her illness.
Because AIDS is often thought of as a fatal disease, some people tend to think of those who have it as 'dying from AIDS' rather than 'living with AIDS'. Everyone with AIDS has the right to live as full a life as possible, just like people without AIDS.

NHAT IS BEING DONE TO HELP?

HIV & AIDS ARE EVERYONE'S PROBLEM. ONLY IF WE ALL PLAY OUR PART WILL THEY BECOME THINGS OF THE PAST.

People are helping in different ways – trying to find a cure for the disease, improving the treatment available to those who have it, and recognising the need to have responsible and sensitive attitudes to the issues.

Because the virus changes its composition constantly, development of a vaccine is a very slow process. Drugs have been made to help people who are HIV positive stay healthy and delay the onset of full-blown AIDS. Although many people with AIDS have to face their situation alone, others find they can rely on the support of other people. One example is 'buddying'. Buddies offer practical support to AIDS sufferers of both sexes. They might help with day to day activities, such as bathing, if a person is too weak to do this alone. They often give emotional support also.

Buddies might become close friends with the person they are buddying for.

▽A week later Joanna still refused to speak to Glen.

IT'S NOT FAIR. WE DIDN'T TELL ANYONE. KIERAN'S USELESS.

YOU SHOULD HEAR THE THINGS HE'S SAYING. WHAT IS HIS PROBLEM?

THAT'S RIGHT. I KNOW SOMEONE WITH AIDS WHOSE NEIGHBOURS TRIED TO HAVE HIM THROWN OUT OF THE BUILDING. THEY WERE FRIGHTENED OF PEOPLE WITH AIDS BECAUSE OF WHAT THE PAPERS SAID.

YOU AND GLEN ARE LUCKY IN SOME WAYS, BECAUSE YOU KNOW MICHAEL AND MAC. LOTS OF PEOPLE DON'T HAVE THE INFORMATION ABOUT HIV YOU HAVE.

△Michael said that at least James and Lizzie had seen sense. They'd invited everyone round next week.

DO YOU THINK THEY'LL EVER FIND A CURE?

IT DOESN'T LOOK LIKELY IN THE NEAR FUTURE, BUT THERE ARE NEW DEVELOPMENTS ALL THE TIME. WE NEVER GIVE UP HOPING.

▽The following day at school Kieran came up to Glen.

SEEN YOUR AIDS GIRLFRIEND TODAY?

WHAT'S YOUR PROBLEM, KIERAN? WHY CAN'T YOU LEAVE HER ALONE?

HOW DID HER MUM GET IT? WAS SHE INJECTING DRUGS OR SOMETHING?

NO, SHE WASN'T. IF YOU'D MET HER YOU'D KNOW SHE'S REALLY NICE.

MAYBE SHE HAD AN AFRICAN BOYFRIEND THEN? THEY SAY THAT'S WHERE IT CAME FROM FIRST OF ALL.

I'M SORRY ABOUT WHAT I SAID. I FOUND OUT IT WASN'T YOU WHO TOLD KIERAN. HIS BROTHER KNOWS A NEIGHBOUR OF OURS.

THINGS ARE BETTER. I SAW THE HEADTEACHER LAST WEEK. SHE KNOWS WHAT'S GOING ON NOW.

THAT'S JUST RACIST RUBBISH KIERAN. YOU'RE SO PREJUDICED.

THAT'S OKAY.

△Glen said the point was that people everywhere were affected by AIDS.

▷After school, Joanna came up to Glen and Anna.

HOW ARE YOU COPING?

△They arranged to go out for the day at the weekend.

Education is one of the most effective measures in the fight against AIDS.
There are books, leaflets, videos and articles available, many aimed at specific people who might be at risk. Certain schemes offer free condoms or needles. Some feel this encourages people to continue to engage in activities which put them at risk. Others say that until the education messages get through, people should be as safe as possible.

Mac knows that more is being learned about AIDS every day.
There is evidence now that AIDS may have existed for decades, but it is only now that it has become such a major problem. It is important to realise that a lot of the information which was given out when HIV & AIDS were first known about might be out of date or not completely accurate. Medical advances are being made all the time. Much more is now understood, but there is still a way to go.

WHAT CAN WE DO?

HAVING READ THIS BOOK, YOU SHOULD KNOW MORE ABOUT HIV & AIDS AND THE EFFECTS THEY CAN HAVE ON PEOPLE'S LIVES.

You will know that you cannot contract the virus through casual contact with people who have HIV or AIDS.

As you grow older, and eventually begin making decisions about your sexual behaviour, you need to be aware of the importance of protecting yourself from possible exposure to the virus. This will include finding out about safer sex, and not letting curiosity or outside influences tempt you into taking unnecessary risks. Remember that although HIV can only be passed on in particular ways, given the right circumstances anyone can contract the virus. Those with HIV or AIDS have an illness. They still have the same needs and wants as anyone else, and should not be discriminated against. You can help by challenging prejudice and misinformation. AIDS is a serious problem, but understanding the issues needn't stop you enjoying the process of growing up. It is a matter of keeping everything in perspective.

The Terence Higgins Trust
52-54 Grays Inn Road
London
WC1X 8JU
Helpline: 0171 831 0330
Their helpline is open to offer practical support, advice, counselling and help to anyone with, or concerned about AIDS.

National AIDS Helpline
Tel: 0800 567123
Free 24 hour confidential services for anyone with questions about HIV and AIDS.

CHILDREN AND YOUNG PEOPLE OFTEN LOOK TO ADULTS FOR GUIDANCE IN DEVELOPING ATTITUDES TOWARDS SERIOUS ISSUES SUCH AS AIDS.

Adults can help by checking their own knowledge of the facts about HIV and AIDS, and their feelings about the subject.
Young people and adults who have read this book together may like to discuss their thoughts and ideas about the issues raised. People who would like more information about any aspect of HIV and AIDS or who would like to talk to someone in confidence can to obtain help, advice and support from the organisations listed below.

Department of Health AIDS Unit
Friars House,
157-168 Blackfriars Road
London
SE1 8EU
Tel: 0171 972 2000

London Lighthouse
111-117 Lancaster Road
London
W11 1QT
Tel: 0171 792 1200

The Samaritans
Local branch numbers will be in the phone directory.

Crusaid
Livingstone House
Carteret Street. London
SW18 9DJ
Tel: 0171 976 8100

AIDS Crisis Trust
38 Ebury Street
London
SE5 0PQ
Tel: 0171 730 0103

Body Positive
51b Philbeach Gardens
London
SW5 9EB
Tel: 0171 373 9124

National Youth Foundation
PO Box 606
Carlingford
New South Wales 2118
Australia
Tel: 00 612 211 1788

Ministry of Youth
PO Box 10-300
Wellington
New Zealand
Tel: 00 644 471 2158

Childline
Freepost 1111
London N1 OBR
Tel 0800 1111

INDEX

Photocredits
All the pictures in this book are by Roger Vlitos apart from pages: 1, 3, 4, 9 bottom, 10, 12 bottom, 15 bottom, 16, 19 top, 22 top, 29 top: Frank Spooner; The publishers wish to acknowledge that all of the photographs taken by Roger Vlitos in this book have been posed by models.